This book belongs to

_____

このほんは

_____

のものです。

Kono hon wa

_____

no mono desu.

Library of Congress Control Number: 2021914311

ebook ISBN 978-1-7368003-0-0
Hardback ISBN 978-1-7368003-1-7
Paperback ISBN 978-1-7368003-2-4

Printed in the United States

First print edition August 2021

Created by Christine Kawabata
Typeset in TaiyoKumo

The Taiyo Kumo logo is a trademark of Taiyo Kumo

San Francisco, California

Taiyo Kumo - Let's try together!
Become a part of our community at www.TaiyoKumo.com
Like us on Facebook @TaiyoAndKumo
Follow us on Instagram @Taiyo.Kumo
Tag us on TikTok @TaiyoAndKumo

For Sophie, Ethan, and Nathaniel

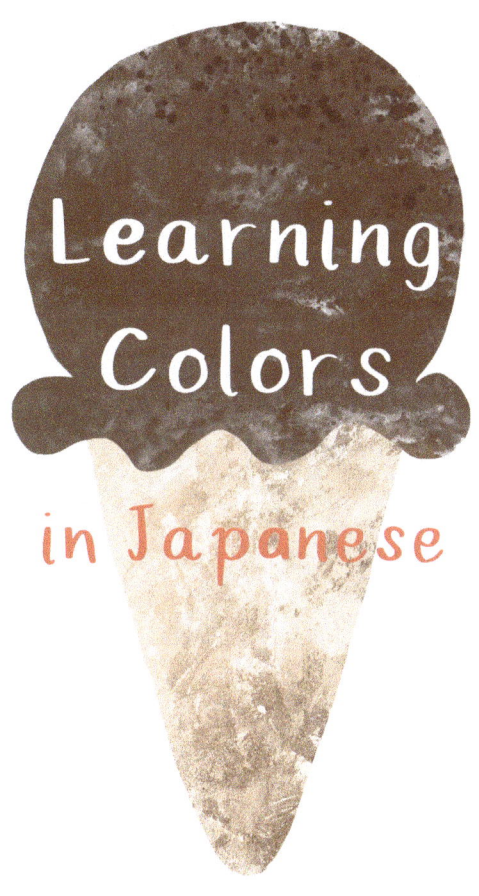

Learning
Colors
in Japanese

by Christine Kawabata

Hi, my name is TaiyO!

I am Kumo...

...Do
you
know
any
colors?

Hmmm...

Do you like
ice cream?

Yes . . .

why?

I have
an

idea!

I'll show you each
color three ways

English

Hiragana
or
Katakana

Romaji

white

しろ

shiro

Ok, let's do it!

Yay! We're all set!

Let's try together!

black

くろ

kuro

grey

グレー

guree

white

しろ

shiro

brown

ちゃいろ

chairo

purple

むらさき

murasaki

blue

あお

ao

green

みどり

midori

yellow

きいろ

kiiro

orange

オレンジ

orenji

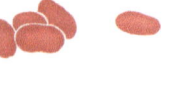

red

あか

aka

pink

ピンク

pinku

Wow, you know
so many colors!

Now you do too!

Let's try
something.

How many
colors

can you name?

Colors

Nice job!

Every time you
try again,
you're going to
learn
a little more!

Thanks!

I also noticed
some fun, tasty things!

Single scoop
One delicious scoop
of ice cream

Double scoop
Two delicious
scoops
of ice cream!

Soft serve
Fun swirls
of
soft serve
ice cream

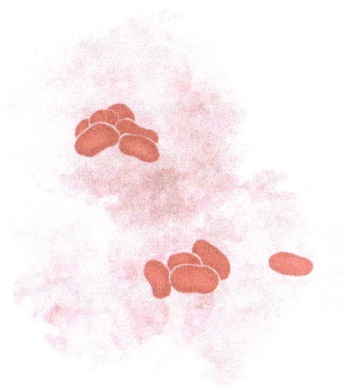

Azuki
red bean
subtly
sweet and
popular
in Japanese
desserts

Kinako
soybean flour
soft, smooth
texture
with a
slightly
toasted,
nutty flavor

Taiyaki
fish shaped
pancake-like
dessert
often filled
with azuki

Sugar cone
sturdy and
crunchy
with a
flat top
and pointy
bottom

Cake cone
light, crispy, and wafer-like with a flat top and flat bottom

Waffle cone
crunchy with a wide mouth and a pointy bottom

Thanks so much!

Learning colors was yummy.

You're fun!

Sure!
We can do
anything
when we
try together!

CHRISTINE KAWABATA

is a Japanese-American author and illustrator living in San Francisco, California with her husband and three kids.

When she was little, she wanted to be a "professional ice cream taster." She hopes fellow aspiring ice cream tasters enjoy learning colors with Taiyo and Kumo!

CPSIA information can be obtained
at www.ICGtesting.com
Printed in the USA
LVHW070933091021
699689LV00013B/5

9 781736 800317